To: Barbara
Happy Mother's Day!
God Bless,
Eddie, Helen & Michelle

D1020225

'95

God
is in
Control

TWILA PARIS

Artist: Victoria Marshall

D7551
ISBN: 0-87162-683-7

Printed in Me
Warner Press,

Like every believer,
I am called to love God above all else
and to live a life of obedience to Him.
My prayer is that God's people
will experience the reality and joy
of a relationship with Jesus Christ
and that they will always hear
His voice above my own.

Twila Paris

God is in control.
How often we need this reminder
as we get caught up in the struggles of daily living.
What peace could be ours if we would only
claim God's power as our source of strength.

In whatever situation you find yourself today—
whether you sing in joy and triumph,
or cry in sorrow and loss—
may you know the all-encompassing love of God.
May you place your life in His care,
lean on His strength,
and discover His everlasting peace.

*T*his is no time for fear;
this is a time for faith
and determination.

*D*on't lose the vision here—
carried away by the motion.

Hold on to all that you
hide in your heart.

There is one thing
that has always been true;
it holds the world together....

God is in control.
We believe
that His children
will not be forsaken.

God is in control.
We will choose
to remember
and never be shaken.

*T*here is no power above
or beside Him.
We know
God is in control.

History marches on;
there is a bottom line
drawn across the ages.

*C*ulture can make its plan;
oh, but the line never changes.

No matter how
the deception may fly,
there is one thing
that has always been true.
It will be true forever....

*H*e has never let you down;
why start to worry now?

He is still the Lord of all we see,
and He is still the loving Father
watching over you and me.

God is in control.
We believe that His children
will not be forsaken.
God is in control.
We will choose to remember
and never be shaken.
There is no power above
or beside Him.
We know God is in control.

"*I* will never leave thee,
nor forsake thee."

HEBREWS 13:5

"*I* am with you always,
even unto the end of the world."

MATTHEW 28:20